Mommy, and me gluten-free!

•Stories and Recipes to Inspire You•

• by Sharon and Alexander Feskanin •

To: Plant your Seed & Bless Children. Joy to you! Sharon Feskanin Proverbs 3:5-6

"He alone is my rock and my salvation: He is my fortress, I will not be shaken." Psalms 62:6 (NIV)

Introduction

*T*his book was written as a testimony of God's presence in our lives. In 2004, our baby boy was diagnosed with extensive food allergies and intolerances. You name it, Alexander's body rejected it. As a result, his strong reactions lead to severe eczema. Although we sought appropriate medical care from several doctors, it became apparent we needed to create our own food for Alexander.

Sharon's passion grew from preparing organic and natural food to creating recipes free from egg, dairy, wheat, or gluten products. For our son's sake, our kitchen became a science lab for experimenting with safe ingredients. We knew Sharon's first recipe was a triumph when we heard our 18-month-old son put his first-ever two words together, "More cookie!" That day not only marked the beginning of a healthy and tasty oatmeal cookie, but many more scrumptious treats.

It's been a long journey to where we are today. Our family has experienced God's faithfulness in more ways than we could imagine. Even through our latest trial of a lengthy unemployment, we know through faith and perseverance we can overcome any obstacle. We know we're not alone. There are many of you who are struggling with similar financial issues or other trying circumstances. In the midst of our battles, Sharon and I have learned to more readily "put on the full armor of God...and take up the shield of faith" (Ephesians 6: 10-18). It's made all the difference.

Sharon's unwavering resolve for Alexander's healing and belief that God uses our struggles for His good are the driving forces behind this book. The recipes we've included are just a sampling of Sharon's expansive menu, born from adversity and necessity. They're the favorites of friends, family members and customers of our home-grown business, Zander's Healthy Bakery, LLC.

Our prayer is when you try a recipe and read its corresponding story and scripture, you'll be inspired in mind, body and spirit. May these gluten-free recipes transform your dessert preferences into healthier choices. May the snapshots from our journey illustrate the presence and love of God in every detail of your life.

We're convinced there's a reason you're holding this book in your hand. We've already prayed for you.

God's many blessings to you and yours,
Ron Feskanin

Acknowledgments

$\mathcal{O}$n October 31, 2009, I heard God call me to write this book, not only to share these recipes but also our life stories with you. At that time, I couldn't understand how this book could come together in such a short time. However, God said that he would send the people and He did.

I deeply express my gratitude for the team that has contributed its time and energy to this book. The book would not be complete without giving a warm honoring to these generous loving people.

My husband Ron, thank you for giving your time and talent to this book. I am thrilled that you had an opportunity to be part of this awesome adventure! And thank you to the following team of family and friends for their dedication and loving attitudes!

Editors: Meridith Kelly, Ron Feskanin, Denise Noble, Emilie Simmons and Paula Jenkins.
Artists: Don and Carol Gray, Andrea Shrote, Paula Jenkins, Ron and Alexander Feskanin.
Graphic Designer: Paula Jenkins
Recipe Testers: Lisa Albritton, Diane Schmidt, Denise Noble, Melinda Lillis, Rachael Riaza, and Carla Jimmerson.
Computer Support: John Schilling, for your willingness to help and bring our computer back to life!

God used two very special people in my life to bring the title of this book "Mommy and Me Gluten-Free" to fruition. I thank you my dear son, Alexander, for your gift to listen to God's voice. Also to my life-long friend, Lisa Albritton, who listened to God speak the words "Mommy and Me Gluten-Free" and your endless support from the beginning of the book's conception.

I have been blessed to have a great sister, Mellody, who is my prayer warrior and supports and believes in the impossible to be the possible. Many thanks to you and Mike for your unconditional support and prayers. God has sent many prayer warriors who have not given up on us in our adversity. I am indebted to these caring and loving people. These prayers have energized my spirit "not to give up" and to move forward to the plans that God has given us to inspire others through recipes and stories.

Most importantly, I give praise to my loving God who is my shelter, my peace, my comforter, my deliverer, my helper, my Everything!

Sharon Feskanin

Table of Contents

"Commit to the Lord whatever you do and your plans will succeed." Proverbs 16:3 (NIV)

Work With What You Got

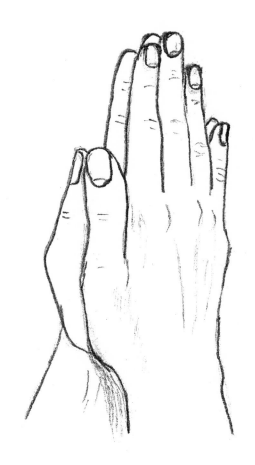

*M*y son Alexander ate his first cookie when he was 18 months old. Prior to experiencing this childhood culinary rite of passage, his eczema, indigestion, and stomach cramps kept the cookie jar out of reach. I spent hours creating a healthy alternative to store bought cookies that inevitably would wreak havoc on his body, already battered by severe food allergies.

I was like a mad scientist experimenting with ingredients that melded together into either a yucky mass of bland or a tasty chunk of heaven. I solicited Ron and some neighbors as taste testers, rolling their comments into new balls of dough until, guided by God's hand, I got it right.

The day before his second birthday, word association came to life as we practiced saying "cookie" while eating one. The size of his smile gauged his pleasure. Obviously motivated and hungry for more after his first bite, he put his first-ever two words together, "more cookie." I knew then my reward for all the time and energy I put into A's Oats & Spice Cookies was Alexander's brilliant smile as he asked for more.

It takes a lot of trial and error to get the measurements of a new recipe just right, but no amount of tries could measure my joy at that moment seven birthdays and 60 allergy-sensitive recipes later.

A's Oats & Spice Cookies
No matter your age, these cookies are guaranteed
to make you smile and ask for more.

Oatmeal Orange Spice Cookie

1. ¾ cup extra virgin olive oil
2. ¾ cup organic sugar
   (Wholesome Sweeteners)
3. ¾ cup sucanat (Wholesome Sweeteners)
4. 2 tablespoons flaxseeds (Bob's Red Mill)
5. ⅔ cup rice milk
6. 3 cups gluten-free oats
   (Bob's Red Mill), finely ground*
7. ¾ cup coconut flour (Bob's Red Mill)
8. 2½ teaspoons cinnamon
9. ¼ teaspoon nutmeg
10. ¼ teaspoon cloves
11. 1 teaspoon vanilla extract
    (Simply Organic)
12. 1½ teaspoons orange oil (Simply Organic)
13. ¾ teaspoon sea salt (Real Salt)
14. 1 teaspoon baking soda
15. 1 cup gluten-free oats (Bob's Red Mill)
16. ¾ cup raisins

Preheat oven to 325°F. Combine ingredients 1 through 3 in order, and mix on medium high speed for 1 minute. NOTE: If using a handheld mixer, place ingredients 4 and 5 in a blender and blend for 1 to 2 minutes. Then mix flaxseed and rice milk mixture with ingredients 1 through 3, and mix on medium high speed for 1 minute.

*Making oat flour: Grind 3 cups oats in food processor or flour mill. This will yield approximately 2½ cups oat flour.

With mixer on, gradually add ingredients 6 and 7 (in order). Mix for 1 to 2 minutes on medium high speed, scraping bowl occasionally. Gradually add ingredients 8 through 14 (in order), and mix on medium speed for 1 minute, scraping bowl occasionally. Slowly add oats and raisins and mix on medium high speed for 1 minute, scraping bowl occasionally.

Use a small (1½ inch) cookie scoop to place cookie dough on parchment paper.

Bake for 12 to 14 minutes. (Bottom of cookie will be lightly browned.)

Makes approximately 6 dozen cookies.

Note: We utilize organic ingredients when available.

This cookie was created for Ron and his love for the traditional chocolate chip cookie. I dedicate this recipe to my loving husband and his love for those cookies!

"Traditional" Chocolate Chip Cookie

1. ¾ cup extra virgin olive oil
2. ¾ cup organic sugar
   (Wholesome Sweeteners)
3. ¾ cup sucanat (Wholesome Sweeteners)
4. 2 tablespoons flaxseeds (Bob's Red Mill)
5. ⅔ cup rice milk
6. 3 cups gluten-free oats
   (Bob's Red Mill), finely ground*
7. 1 teaspoon baking soda
8. ¾ teaspoon sea salt (Real Salt)
9. 1 teaspoon vanilla extract
   (Simply Organic)
10. ¾ cup coconut flour (Bob's Red Mill)
11. ¾ cup semi-sweet chocolate chips
    (Enjoy Life)

$\mathcal{P}$reheat oven to 325°F. Combine ingredients 1 through 3 in order and mix on medium high speed for 1 minute. NOTE: If using a handheld mixer, place ingredients 4 and 5 in a blender and blend well for 1 to 2 minutes. Then mix flaxseed and rice milk mixture with ingredients 1 through 3, and mix on medium high speed for 1 minute, scraping bowl occasionally.

*Making oat flour: Place 3 cups oats in food processor or flour mill and process oats to flour consistency. This will yield about 2 ½ cups oat flour.

Gradually add ingredients 6 through 10 (in order). Mix for 1 to 2 minutes on medium high speed, scraping bowl occasionally. Mix well, then turn mixer on medium high and add chocolate chips.

Use a small (1½ inch) cookie scoop and place cookie dough on parchment paper on cookie sheet.

Bake for 12 to 14 minutes. (Bottom of cookies will be lightly browned.)

Makes approximately 6 dozen cookies.

Storage Tip: A Chewy Cookie – Store in a closed plastic container.
A Crunchy Cookie – Store in a paper bag.

Note: We utilize organic ingredients when available.

"You, Oh God, keep my lamp burning. My God turns my darkness into light." Psalms 18:28 (NIV)

Shine on Even When You Don't Feel Like It

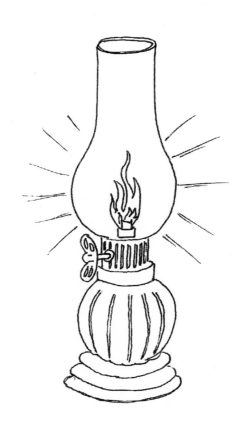

$\mathcal{J}$esus tells us in Matthew 5:16 to "let your light shine bright before men, that they may see your good deeds and praise your Father in heaven." Kilowatts abound during good seasons in life, but when times turn tough, it's a challenge to keep the bulb, called my life, bright.

Most of us have a "happy place" where we're at our brightest, most content, and at peace. Mine is the kitchen, aka "Laboratory." It's also my sanctuary, a place to make my requests known to God as I make edible elixirs for my son. When I turn on the mixer, something connects to my spirit to help me regain some of the brightness I've lost.

Alexander was at a frustrating stage where he didn't want to read or do any of his schoolwork. The battle was bigger than me, so during a nightly kitchen prayer vigil, I asked for God's help and encouragement. I needed some light in my darkness, so while I conjured up a recipe we could share over breakfast, I prayed God would stir up a desire in Alexander to read.

"Cookies for breakfast?" It was not so much a question from Alexander as a statement of wonderment as he walked past the fresh batch. After he ate his fill and with no prompting from me, he marched up to his room and started reading. Later, he announced his desire to read more. A new day brought new light to my struggle with my son. Hope was revealed as a tasty cookie was created.

Ask God to show you how to shine even on days when you feel dimly lit. From my experience, a power surge comes when I turn my gaze toward God and start serving others. We are the light of the world.

I love King David's transparency as he cried out to God: "Oh Lord, hear my prayer, hear my cry for mercy. In your faithfulness and righteousness, come to my relief." (Psalm 143:1) Time after time, God came through for David.

Oatmeal Chocolate Chip Cookie
"Breakfast Cookie"

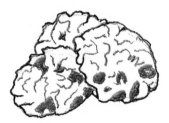

1. ½ cup extra virgin olive oil
2. 1 cup organic raw blue agave (Wholesome Sweeteners)
3. 2 tablespoons flaxseeds (Bob's Red Mill)
4. ⅔ cup rice milk
5. 3½ cups gluten-free oats (Bob's Red Mill), finely ground*
6. 1 cup amaranth flour (Bob's Red Mill)
7. 1 teaspoon vanilla extract (Simply Organic)
8. ¾ teaspoon sea salt (Real Salt)
9. 1 teaspoon baking soda
10. 3½ cups gluten-free oats (Bob's Red Mill)
11. 1 cup pecans, finely ground
12. 1 10-ounce bag semi-sweet chocolate chips (Enjoy Life)

Preheat oven to 325°F. Combine ingredients 1 through 4 in order, and mix on medium high speed for 2 minutes. NOTE: If using a handheld mixer, place ingredients 1 through 4 in a blender and blend well for 1 to 2 minutes. Transfer mixture to mixing bowl.

*Making oat flour: Grind 3 ½ cups oats in food processor or flour mill. This will yield approximately 3 cups oat flour.

With mixer on, gradually add ingredients 5 and 6 in order, and mix for 2 minutes on medium high speed, scraping bowl occasionally. Gradually add ingredients 7 through 9 and mix on medium speed for 1 minute, scraping bowl occasionally. Gradually add ingredients 10 through 12 and mix on medium high speed for 1 to 2 minutes, scraping bowl occasionally.

Please note: Cookie dough will not be "runny" – if it is, mix longer. Also, grains soak up liquids very quickly, so do not let mixture sit. Make cookies immediately to ensure ideal texture.

Use a small (1½ inch) cookie scoop and place cookie dough about 2 inches apart on parchment paper on cookie sheet.

Bake for 8 to 10 minutes. (Bottom of cookies will be lightly browned).

Makes approximately 7 dozen cookies.

Note: We utilize organic ingredients when available.

Alexander's Top 10 Ways to Eat a Breakfast Cookie

 Add an Oatmeal Chocolate Chip Breakfast Cookie on top of vanilla yogurt. My favorite yogurt is Redwood Hills Farm vanilla goat yogurt.

Take breakfast cookies with you to school and share with friends.

 Top your favorite chocolate or vanilla ice cream with an Oatmeal Chocolate Chip Cookie. My favorite is Chocolate Rice Dream.

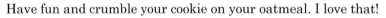

Have fun and crumble your cookie on your oatmeal. I love that!

 Crumble 2 or more Oatmeal Chocolate Chip Cookies on top of fresh strawberries. I can't get enough of this!

Add 2 yummy toppings to our brownie recipes. A scoop of your favorite ice cream and an Oatmeal Chocolate Chip Cookie crumbled on top.

How about a Banana Chocolate Smoothie? Here is our family's recipe. Add an Oatmeal Chocolate Chip Cookie for extra great taste!

Banana Chocolate Smoothie
2 cups rice milk
2 frozen bananas
1 tablespoon raw honey
1 tablespoon unsweetened cocoa powder

Directions: Mom measures all the ingredients and I help with some of them. I place all the ingredients into the blender and turn it on. When I see that it is all together, I turn the mixer off and mom pours the smoothies into our cups and I crumble the cookie on top! I take a spoon to eat the cookie crumbles on top! It tastes so good!

Banana Coconut Delight
Here is a dish Mom likes for breakfast: 1 banana, 1 tablespoon dehydrated coconut slices, and an Oatmeal Chocolate Chip Cookie crumbled on top.

Snack Break
1 cup sunflower seeds, cup raisins, and 3 crumbled Oatmeal Chocolate Chip Cookies. Put all these ingredients in a plastic bag. Pull out the bag when you are ready for a snack break.

My last suggestion is just to enjoy it as part of your breakfast. Yes, have a Breakfast Cookie for breakfast like I do!

"It has been planted in good soil by abundant water so that it would produce branches, bear fruit and become a splendid vine." Ezekiel 17:8 (NJV)

Tiny Garden, Big Blessings

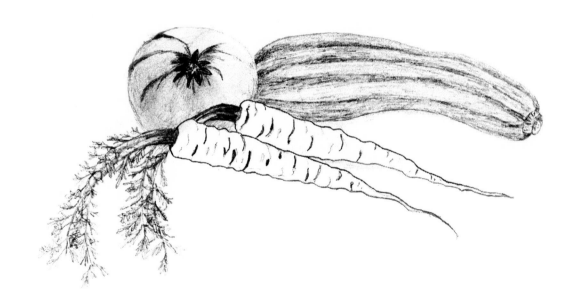

$\mathcal{A}$lexander wanted to create a new soup recipe, but our grocery budget was limited from being unemployed. Since ingredients for a hearty soup were slim pickings, Alexander asked if he could use some vegetables from our "Tiny Garden."

Surrounded by woods and shade, we managed to grow many different vegetables and herbs in a garden about the size of a cemetery plot. Alexander spent many hours entertained by the toads, butterflies and lizards around this meager 4' x 8' slice of land. It's even inspired him to write several short stories about his garden adventures. This time, however, he was on a mission to pick the right vegetables and herbs to stir into a hot pot of broth. He got the affirmation he deserved at dinner that night. From a small garden, came a big blessing: a delicious and filling meal.

Our "Tiny Garden" has brought much joy in our hard times. In spite of its size, the garden is plentiful, providing sustenance in abundance. Could it be God blessed this garden so we could bless others? Alexander sees our harvest shared with others even when we're in need. I want him to see that even in our insufficiency, God's grace is sufficient. As Jesus promised, "my power is made perfect in weakness."

In times of slim pickings, big blessings from small gardens are bountiful indeed.

Garden Soup

1. 32 ounces chicken or vegetable broth
2. 2 carrots, chopped
3. ¼ cup onion, chopped
4. 1 zucchini, chopped
5. ½ teaspoon fresh oregano (if using dried oregano, shake bottle 5 times)
6. ½ teaspoon fresh basil (if using dried basil, shake bottle 5 times)
7. Pinch of salt

J get out a saucepan. I bring out the ingredients. Mom cuts up the vegetables. I pour the broth in the saucepan. Mom turns the stove on medium high. I add the chopped vegetables and herbs. I wait a few minutes to let it boil, then Mom turns the burner down. I wait for the soup to cook for about 5 minutes. That's it! Mom gets the bowls ready and I pour the soup in the bowl. This is yummy. Hope you love it, too.

The Garden Burglars

Alexander Feskanin

Once upon a time there were garden burglars.
They were in the garden to steal tomatoes.
Meanwhile, the Toad Police were after them.
The leader of the tomato worms was the eater
of the leaves. The Toad Police saw the worms,
then drew their swords and the worms did too.
Then they crashed their swords in to each other's
swords. There was loud crashing: CLANG! CLANG!
CLANG! The police won the battle and took the
garden burglars (tomato worms) to jail.

The End

"A generous man will prosper; he who refreshes others will himself be refreshed." Proverbs 11:25 (NIV)

Farmer Muffins

I drove home on a late spring day thinking how great it would be to purchase some fresh produce from a local farm. As I passed by a farm near our home, I noticed two men out in the field and felt led to stop. I explained to the farmers that I was working on some recipes and in need of fresh veggies that we couldn't grow. The farmer who owned the property agreed to contact me when the vegetables were ready to be harvested. He remained true to his word.

Little did I know, that detour would be the beginning of a great friendship. Since then, Alexander and I have enjoyed visiting the farm and showering his animals with love and attention. Sadly, our farmer friend was diagnosed with diabetes. After expressing he'd love to have some of my homemade muffins, I decided to experiment with some unusual ingredients to help keep his sugar levels in a healthy range. It wasn't until our farmer friend dropped off some bananas and fresh Georgia pecans that things came together to create a low-glycemic muffin.

After many attempts, the Banana Pecan Muffins finally passed the taste inspection. How fulfilling it was to hear the muffins were not only good, but didn't affect his sugar levels. Occasionally, he drops a hint and leaves ripe bananas by our door, but his generosity isn't tainted with expectations of getting anything in return.

Regardless, it's fun to swap blessings with each other without saying a word. There's a mutual gratitude for each other's gifts. His gift is producing a bountiful buffet of veggies for us to enjoy, and mine is baking delectable muffins meeting his special need. Our skills, talents and gifts are meant to be shared.

Banana Pecan Muffins

1. **2 cups banana puree (approximately 1½ lbs. very ripe bananas pureed in food processor to achieve "smoothie" consistency)**
2. **½ cup canola oil**
3. **¼ cup flaxseed meal (Bob's Red Mill)**
4. **½ cup rice milk**
5. **¾ cup organic raw blue agave (Wholesome Sweeteners)**
6. **2 teaspoons vanilla extract (Simply Organic)**
7. **2 cups brown rice flour (Bob's Red Mill)**
8. **2 teaspoons baking powder**
9. **1 teaspoon baking soda**
10. **½ teaspoon salt**
11. **½ cup tapioca flour**
12. **1 cup pecans, minced**

Variation: Add ¼ to ½ cup semi-sweet chocolate chips (Enjoy Life)

Preheat oven to 350°F. Mix ingredients 1 through 5 (add in order) for 1 minute on medium high speed. Gradually add ingredients 6 through 8 (in order), and mix on medium speed, scraping bowl occasionally. Add ingredients 9 through 11 (in order), and mix on medium high speed for 1 minute. Add pecans on medium high speed. Blend well.

Pour batter into muffin pan. (An ice cream scoop works well to place batter in pan.)

Bake for 15 to 18 minutes or until lightly browned. Place pan on cooling rack, and cool for at least 30 minutes.

Allow muffins to refrigerate for a few hours to develop optimal taste. We love these right out of the refrigerator!

Makes approximately 18 muffins.

Note: We utilize organic ingredients when available.

"I prayed for this child, and the Lord has granted me what I asked of Him." 1 Samuel 1:27 (NIV)

The Best Mother's Day Ever

$\mathcal{M}$other's Day was the ultimate reminder of what we were living without the gift of a child. As others were getting corsages and standing in honor from their church pew, I was on the outside looking in on a dream denied. To me, Mother's Day was nothing but a hurtful reminder of our infertility struggles. Each May, I felt intentionally left out of the celebration of motherhood and hoped the next year would be different. As selfish as that sounds, it was me being vulnerable and real. I'm grateful God encourages authenticity as we approach His throne.

After six years of May passed, we refocused our prayers in January 2002. Open to adoption, the doors of parenthood swung wide open nine months later. Ron and I received our baby announcement one week before Alexander's birth. As we scurried to get ready for our baby boy, we rejoiced knowing we had loved him for years in our longings and prayers. It was a worthy wait. God wastes nothing.

Flash forward several Mother's Days later to one of the best. The banging from the kitchen captured my imagination. I wondered what Alexander was doing before his normal wake up time. I restrained from getting out of bed as to not ruin the "surprise." I could track Alexander's every move from my bed from his retrieving a stepstool to reach high cabinets to his trek to the basement for a breakfast tray.

Alexander appeared at my bedroom door with a tray adorned with toast, water and a few of my favorite Banana Coconut Muffins. "Mom I didn't think about myself once this morning. I was only thinking about you." It was wondrous to hear those selfless words come from a child God entrusted to us after years of longing. Alexander's words reflect Christ's disposition toward us not just on Mother's Day, but every day. He never stops thinking about us.

Banana Coconut Muffins

1. **2 cups banana puree (approximately 1½ lbs. very ripe bananas pureed in food processor to achieve "smoothie" consistency)**
2. **½ cup canola oil**
3. **¼ cup flaxseed meal (Bob's Red Mill)**
4. **¾ cup coconut milk**
5. **½ cup organic raw blue agave (Wholesome Sweeteners)**
6. **2 teaspoons vanilla extract (Simply Organic)**
7. **2 cups brown rice flour (Bob's Red Mill)**
8. **½ teaspoon salt**
9. **2 teaspoons baking powder**
10. **1 teaspoon baking soda**
11. **¼ cup coconut flour (Bob's Red Mill)**
12. Dehydrated coconut flakes, or unsweetened coconut flakes

$\mathcal{P}$reheat oven to 350°F. Combine ingredients 1 through 5 (add in order), and mix for 1 minute on medium high speed. Gradually add ingredients 6 through 8 (in order), and mix on medium speed for 1 minute, scraping bowl occasionally. Add ingredients 9 through 11 (in order), and mix on medium high speed for 1 minute. Make sure ingredients are blended well.

Pour batter into muffin pan. (An ice cream scoop works well to place batter in pan.) Sprinkle coconut flakes on top.

Bake for 15 to 18 minutes or until lightly browned.

Place pan on cooling rack, and cool for at least 30 minutes. Allow muffins to refrigerate for a few hours to develop optimal taste. We love these right out of the refrigerator!

Makes approximately 18 muffins.

Note: We utilize organic ingredients when available.

"Let them praise his name with dancing and make music to him with tambourine and harp." Psalm 149:3 (NJV)

Praise Him with a Dance

$\mathcal{G}$od's an amazing architect of people and situations to help meet us at the point of our deepest need. As we float along lost in despair, disappointment or disillusionment, we look up and find there are others in the same boat to help us find The Way.

Alexander and I dedicated ourselves to pray for the unemployed. Our prayer list included a friend's husband who also struggled with a lengthy unemployment. We understood their anxiousness and each day would lift them up, along with other families and our own, to God's care. After a long wait, we received the good news. Her husband landed a "miracle job" the same executive position at the same company he resigned from three years earlier!

I was honored to give thanks with her and be a part of the answer through faithful intercession. Without any inhibitions, I danced with joy knowing though we may wait, God will provide. Doing "immeasurably more than all we ask or imagine" is a specialty of the God of the universe. The look on Alexander's face was priceless as he saw his mom flailing about in the living room. It didn't take long before he joined the dance.

To commemorate their joy, Alexander and I made Banana Chocolate Muffins for my friend and her newly employed husband. Before you partake of these decadent muffins, do a little jig. Praise God for overcoming your challenging circumstances, even if it hasn't happened yet. Remember, He's the same God who has overcome the world.

Banana Chocolate Muffins

1. 2 cups banana puree (approximately 1½ lbs. very ripe bananas pureed in food processor to achieve "smoothie" consistency)
2. ½ cup unsweetened cocoa powder (Now® Foods)
3. ½ cup canola oil
4. ¼ cup flaxseed meal (Bob's Red Mill)
5. ¾ cup rice milk
6. ½ cup organic raw blue agave (Wholesome Sweeteners)
7. 2 teaspoons vanilla extract (Simply Organic)
8. 2 cups brown rice flour (Bob's Red Mill)

9. 2 teaspoons baking powder
10. 1 teaspoon baking soda
11. ½ teaspoon salt
12. ½ cup unsweetened baking cocoa
13. ¼ - ½ cup semi-sweet chocolate chips (Enjoy Life)

Preheat oven to 350°. Combine ingredients 1 through 5 (add in order), and mix for 1 minute on medium high speed. Gradually blend in ingredients 6 through 8 (add in order), and mix on medium speed, scraping bowl occasionally. Add ingredients 9 through 11 (in order), and mix on medium high speed for 1 minute. Blend well. Stir in baking chips.

Pour batter into muffin pan. (An ice cream scoop works well to place batter in pan.)

Bake for 15 to 18 minutes or until lightly browned. Place pan on cooling rack, and cool for at least 30 minutes.

Allow muffins to refrigerate for a few hours to develop optimal taste. We love these right out of the refrigerator!

Alternative ingredient for semi-sweet chocolate chips - Raw Chocolate Nibs (also known as Cacao).

Makes approximately 18 muffins.

Note: We utilize organic ingredients when available.

Then the Lord said to Moses, "I will rain down bread from heaven for you. The people are to go out each day and gather enough for that day." Exodus 16:4 (NIV)

Manna from Heaven

$\mathcal{T}$o add insult to injury on an already anxious morning, we had run out of bread. Under normal circumstances running out of groceries isn't a killjoy, but after six months of unemployment my usual cheerful morning demeanor was replaced with discouragement. I had allowed circumstances to compromise my joy. A little nuisance was defining my day.

We could barely cover necessities and six dollars for bread was a humble stretch. I began to question God's ability to meet our needs since a few dollars had become such a large sum in the midst of our financial distress. The petition to "give us today our daily bread" seemed more like a test of faith than a model for prayer. But, after considering the track record of God, I took Him at His word and asked.

A friend called after I had returned from the tearful trip to the grocery store with two loaves of bread. I recapped my morning admitting how a breadless kitchen sent me down a fretful path. Remarkably, my friend had spent the morning baking bread and wanted to deliver some loaves to me. "Sharon, you'll never run out of bread." In my heart I could hear God whisper the same words spoken so gently by my loving friend. He had doubled our bread status in a matter of minutes.

That same day another friend told me she had something to drop off at my house. What was the "something?" You guessed it, more bread. It was fresh, right-out-of-the-oven cranberry bread from a friend who didn't even know the first. I laughed at God's sense of humor and accepted my personal manna from heaven with open arms and a grateful heart.

What is it you need God to provide for you today? Is it strength, perseverance, healing, a forgiving heart, or something as simple as a loaf of Banana Bread? I peeked into my refrigerator that night and chuckled at my generous supply of what was nonexistent at the beginning of the day.

Deluxe Petite Banana Bread

1. **2 cups banana puree (approximately 1½ lbs. very ripe bananas pureed in food processor to achieve "smoothie" consistency)**
2. **½ cup canola oil**
3. **¼ cup flaxseed meal (Bob's Red Mill)**
4. **½ cup rice milk**
5. **¾ cup organic raw blue agave (Wholesome Sweeteners)**
6. **2 teaspoons vanilla extract (Simply Organic)**
7. **2 cups brown rice flour (Bob's Red Mill)**
8. **2 teaspoons baking powder**
9. **1 teaspoon baking soda**
10. **½ teaspoon salt**
11. **½ cup tapioca flour**
12. **1 cup pecans, finely ground**
13. **½ cup semi-sweet chocolate chips (Enjoy Life)**
14. **Dehydrated coconut flakes, or medium shredded coconut flakes**

*P*reheat oven to 350°F. Gradually mix ingredients 1 through 5 (add in order) for 1 minute on medium high speed. Gradually blend in ingredients 6 through 8 (add in order), and mix on medium speed, scraping bowl occasionally. Add ingredients 9 through 11 (in order), and mix on medium high speed for 1 minute. Add pecans and chocolate chips, and mix on medium high speed.

Pour into petite bread mold pan. (You can buy petite bread mold pans and petite baking liners at Hobby Lobby. Wilton brand pans hold 9 petite bread molds.) An ice cream scoop works well to place batter in pan. Add dehydrated coconut flakes on top.

Bake for 15 to 18 minutes or until lightly browned. Place pan on cooling rack, and cool for at least 30 minutes.

Allow breads to refrigerate for a few hours to develop optimal taste. We love these right out of the refrigerator!

Makes 18 petite breads.

Note: We utilize organic ingredients when available.

"A cheerful look brings joy to the heart, and good news gives health to the bones." Proverbs 15:30 (NIV)

You Can Make a Cupcake with those Ingredients?

Delicious and healthy desserts are never in short supply at our house when there's something to celebrate. A few years ago, while Alexander was attending a homeschool lab, I eagerly volunteered to deliver some of my "celebratory sweetness" to his classmates.

I'm always up to the dessert-making task, especially when I know a recipient has to bear the burden of living with "special dietary needs." I found out one of Alexander's classmates also had food allergies. Since my son's allergies were so severe, I learned to create recipes mirroring common foods with uncommon ingredients.

I kept his classmate's list of food restrictions in mind as I made Banana Cupcakes topped with a special icing. As a consumption test, I ran the ingredients by the child's mom. "You can make a cupcake with those ingredients?" Her bewilderment turned to encouragement as I shared how we overcame our food allergy struggles by being creative with food.

I'll never forget the day I brought the cupcakes to Alexander's class. To be able to eat what everyone else was eating was a blessing to his classmate. Sweet satisfaction came over me as I watched her jump up and down with excitement. It was Christmas morning on a school day.

Here's to that little girl and many others I've encountered with special dietary needs. May you eat these cupcakes and my other creations without a care in the world. Go ahead, jump!

Banana Cupcakes

1. **2 cups banana puree (approximately 1½ lbs. very ripe bananas pureed in food processor to achieve "smoothie" consistency)**
2. **½ cup canola oil**
3. **¼ cup flaxseed meal (Bob's Red Mill)**
4. **½ cup rice milk**
5. **1 cup organic sugar (Wholesome Sweeteners)**
6. **2 teaspoons vanilla extract (Simply Organic)**
7. **2 cups brown rice flour (Bob's Red Mill)**
8. **2 teaspoons baking powder**
9. **1 teaspoon baking soda**
10. **½ teaspoon salt**
11. **½ cup tapioca flour**

Preheat oven to 350°F. Combine ingredients 1 through 5 (add in order), and mix for 1 minute on medium high speed. Gradually add ingredients 6 through 8 (in order), and mix on medium speed for 1 minute, scraping bowl occasionally. Add ingredients 9 through 11 (in order), and mix on medium high speed for 1 minute. Blend ingredients well.

Fill muffin cups ¾ full. (An ice cream scoop works well to place batter in muffin pan).

Bake for 15 to 18 minutes or until lightly browned.

Place pan on cooling rack, and cool for at least 30 minutes.

Add vanilla or chocolate icing. (See page 82 for icing recipe.) If using chocolate icing, add ½ cup chocolate baking chips in cupcake batter. This is highly kid-approved!

Makes approximately 18 cupcakes.

Note: We utilize organic ingredients when available.

"For the jar of flour was not used up and the jug of oil did not run dry, in keeping with the word of the Lord spoken by Elijah." 1 Kings 17:16 (NIV)

Pour Out the Blessings

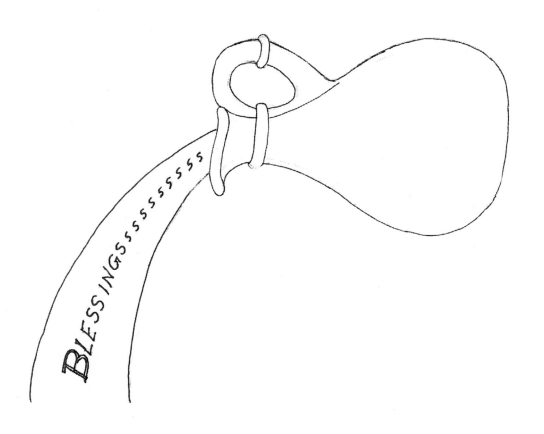

BLESSINGSssssssssss

J sure could use a commercial mixer. With family finances tight, necessities trumped luxuries. Five days before Christmas my husband got the ominous news his company was shutting its doors with a mere 10 minute notice. With little time to mentally process the news, these words sprang from my heart: "I'm going to roll out the dough."

Unleashing the power of an electric mixer in my kitchen would enable me to make more "dough" for my recipes and family! So my sister, niece and I faced adversity head-on by unleashing the power of God through prayer. A trivial request? Perhaps, but not to me. To me, a mixer meant provision for my family. Rest assured; God hears all our needs from restoring broken relationships, providing jobs for the unemployed, to accelerating my mixing speed.

Three weeks later, I got a phone call from an acquaintance, who couldn't have possibly known about my appliance petition. She told me she felt led to bless me with a professional grade mixer. Without hesitation, I accepted.

Now, every time I see the gleaming mixing machine on my countertop, I'm reminded of God's goodness. He's not a cosmic Costco, but I believe He loves to bless His children from His vast storehouses, even if it's a mixer from a friend of a friend. He pays attention to every request. In other words, He specializes in giving professional grade mixers to amateurs like me.

As I began my gluten-free journey of faith, my sister and friend prayed I would never run out of oil. While experimenting with Raspberry Squares, I noticed I was low on coconut oil. Unexpectedly, a friend called to invite me to her home. When I arrived, she greeted me with a basketful of cooking supplies. "Here are some goodies I think you'll enjoy." Included in the basket was coconut oil.

Unbeknownst to my friend, God used her generosity to replenish my supply. The prayer that I would never run out of oil miraculously was answered. As soon as I got home I picked up the phone to call my sister and friend. They needed to know their prayer for plenty was in keeping with the word of the Lord. My oil did not run dry.

Raspberry Squares

1. **1 cup unrefined coconut oil, melted*** (Garden of Life)
2. **½ cup organic sucanat** (Wholesome Sweeteners)
3. **1 cup brown rice flour** (Bob's Red Mill)
4. **¼ cup coconut flour** (Bob's Red Mill)
5. **2 tablespoons flaxseed meal** (Bob's Red Mill)
6. **2 teaspoons vanilla extract** (Simply Organic)
7. **½ teaspoon baking soda**
8. **¼ teaspoon sea salt** (Real Salt)
9. **2 cups gluten-free oats** (Bob's Red Mill)
10. **¾ cup unsweetened shredded coconut** (Bob's Red Mill)
11. **1 10-ounce jar raspberry fruit spread** (Cascadian Farm)

Preheat oven to 280°F. Spray 9 x 13-inch baking dish with canola oil. Combine melted coconut oil and sucanat, and mix for 1 minute on medium high speed. Gradually add ingredients 3 through 8, and mix on medium high speed for 1 minute, scraping bowl occasionally. Add oats. Mix on high speed for 1 to 2 minutes.

*Melt coconut oil in saucepan on low heat, then add to mixer.

Press mixture onto bottom of dish. Spread the fruit spread on top. Sprinkle top with coconut.

Bake for 10 to 12 minutes.

Let squares cool for 1 hour, then cut into 18 squares or desired size. Place pan in freezer for 1 hour, take out squares and place them on parchment paper in a sealed plastic container. For an extra touch of elegance, place a raspberry square in a petite paper liner.

Variation: Try apricot fruit spread, too.

Note: We utilize organic ingredients when available.

"Many are asking, 'Who can show us any good?'
Let the light of your face shine upon us,
O Lord." Psalms 4:6 (NIV)

The Lighthouse

$\mathcal{T}$he doctors gave us little hope my mom would survive her near-fatal car accident. The odds weren't stacked in our favor since she was older and suffered severe injuries. But we didn't trust in odds, we trusted in God.

Family members from around the country gathered around her hospital bed while she was in a coma to ask God for healing. My uncle prayed, "God please bring Neva back to us and let her 'lighthouse' smile shine again."

After weeks of medical care, hospital vigils and impromptu prayer meetings, Mom regained consciousness. During the third month of her stay, we celebrated her 74th birthday. I wanted to prepare some birthday treats to make this hospital-bound birthday special, but I was 900 miles away from my kitchen in Atlanta. So I did the only thing I knew to do, pray. God answered through a member of mom's church who graciously allowed me to commandeer her kitchen.

I baked and cooked halfway through the night to prep for the birthday celebration. The following day I took a plate of Apricot Squares to mom. She was delighted to have her favorite dessert, and even more delighted to have us together on a birthday she wasn't expected to celebrate. As mom lit up the sterile room with her "lighthouse" smile, I thought about my uncle's prayer several months earlier. The "Happy Birthday" song never sounded so sweet.

Apricot Squares
(no sweetener added)

1. 1 cup unrefined coconut oil, melted* (Garden of Life)
2. ½ cup dates, finely chopped
3. ½ cup dried apricots, finely chopped
4. ½ cup raw sliced almonds
5. 1 cup brown rice flour (Bob's Red Mill)
6. ¼ cup coconut flour (Bob's Red Mill)
7. 2 tablespoons flaxseed meal (Bob's Red Mill)
8. 2 teaspoons vanilla extract (Simply Organic)
9. ½ teaspoon baking soda
10. ¼ teaspoon sea salt (Real Salt)
11. 2 cups gluten-free oats (Bob's Red Mill)
12. ¾ cup unsweetened shredded coconut (Bob's Red Mill)
13. 1 10-ounce jar apricot fruit spread (Cascadian Farm)

Preheat oven to 280°F. Spray 9 x 13-inch baking dish with canola oil. Combine ingredients 1 through 3, and mix for 1 minute on medium high speed. Gradually add ingredients 4 through 10, and mix on medium high speed for 1 minute, scraping bowl occasionally. Add oats. Mix on high speed for 1 to 2 minutes. Blend well.

*Melt coconut oil in a saucepan on low, then add to mixer.

Press mixture onto bottom of dish. Spread fruit spread on top. Sprinkle top with coconut.

Bake for 12 to 15 minutes.

Let squares cool for 1 hour, then cut into 18 squares or desired size. Remove squares and place them on parchment paper in a sealed plastic container. Refrigerate or freeze. For an extra touch of elegance, place an apricot square in a petite paper liner. They look and taste great!

Note: We utilize organic ingredients when available.

"Good will comes to him who is generous and lends freely, who conducts his affairs with justice." Psalm 112:5 (NIV)

Turning Lemons into Lemon Cookies

Dr. Karl and Sandy

$\mathcal{J}$t was an emotional morning when our dog Sandy had a benign tumor removed. We wondered how he would make it through the procedure, as a pre-existing condition didn't allow for anesthesia. Anyone with a pet understands how deep the attachment runs, so we started a prayer chain the morning of Sandy's operation.

Our veterinarian, Dr. Karl, found another skin growth during surgery. He called to ask permission to remove it, but sadly we didn't have the money to cover another procedure. After explaining our financial situation, Dr. Karl agreed to remove the growth at no cost. I cried tears of joy as I hung up the phone. God was taking care of our beloved dog.

As a show of gratitude, Alexander drew a picture for Dr. Karl. I followed my natural instinct and baked. We surveyed the pantry and refrigerator looking for ingredients for a new cookie for Dr. Karl and found lemons. Lemon Cookies it is! Alexander found the perfect cookie cutter for the occasion. The dog-shaped cookies and picture were a big hit. Dr. Karl's gratitude ran deep and so did ours when we saw Sandy. Our dog was doing well and ready to come home.

Alexander's picture reminds us of the goodness shown to us through the compassion and generosity of Dr. Karl. It exemplifies the debt to Dr. Karl we couldn't pay and the glorious grace that covered it, an illustration of Christ's sacrificial love. The picture is still hanging in his office to this day.

Lemon Shape Cookies

1. **1 cup refined organic coconut oil, melted***
2. **½ cup organic sugar (Wholesome Sweeteners)**
3. **½ cup organic sucanat (Wholesome Sweeteners)**
4. **2 tablespoons flaxseeds (Bob's Red Mill)**
5. **⅓ cup rice milk**
6. **2 teaspoons lemon peel**
7. **2 tablespoons freshly squeezed lemon juice**
8. **2 teaspoons lemon oil (Simply Organic)**
9. **1 cup amaranth flour (Bob's Red Mill)**
10. **1 tablespoon arrowroot starch (Bob's Red Mill)**
11. **½ teaspoon sea salt (Real Salt)**
12. **½ teaspoon baking soda**
13. **3½ cups gluten-free oats (Bob's Red Mill), finely ground****

Combine ingredients 1 through 5 in order, then mix 1 minute on medium high speed. (Mixture will have "glazed" appearance.) Add ingredients 6 through 8, and mix on medium high speed for 1 minute. Gradually add amaranth flour. Mix well, scraping sides when needed. Add ingredients 10 through 12. Mix well. Gradually add oat flour and mix on medium high speed for 1 to 2 minutes. You cannot over-mix this mixture.

*Melt coconut oil in a saucepan on low, then add to mixer.

**Making oat flour: Grind 3 ½ cups oats in food processor or flour mill. This will yield approximately 3 cups oat flour.

Place soft dough in plastic sealed container and refrigerate for 2 to 3 hours until dough is solid.

Preheat oven to 375°F. Roll dough ½-inch thick on floured surface. To prevent dough from sticking to rolling pin, spray canola oil cooking spray on rolling pin. Cut with a 3-inch cookie cutter. Place cookies on parchment paper on cookie sheet about 2 inches apart.

Bake for 10 to 12 minutes. (Bottom of cookies will be slightly browned.) Cool cookies for 1 hour. Spread lemon icing on top of each cookie. See page 82 for icing recipe.

Makes 3 to 4 dozen cookies, depending on thickness of cookie and size of cookie cutter.

Store in a tightly sealed container lined with parchment paper. Refrigerate to ensure freshness. These cookies freeze very well, too.

Note: We utilize organic ingredients when available.

"He who gives to the poor will lack nothing."
Proverbs 28:27 (NIV)

He's Got You Covered

$\mathcal{A}$ friend struggled financially after the death of her husband, so much so that a $12 nutritional item she needed was a major pinch. Despite being in a similar financial situation, I felt God wanted me to purchase this item on her behalf. So off to the store I went.

As I reached into my purse for the money, I was pleasantly surprised I had just the right amount of cash. Even though I was spending all the money I had, I felt a peace only God could give. I believed the words of the Apostle Paul that "my God will meet all my needs according to his glorious riches in Christ Jesus." (Philippians 4:19)

When I got home, a friend called to order $10 worth of Lemon Sandwich Cookies. The timing was amazing – not only was it right after a holiday when business is notoriously slow, but my inventory of lemon cookies were worth exactly $10. I started to cry. I explained how God used her to help cover a recent expense. She was thrilled to be part of the blessing. After I hung up the phone, I went to get the mail. My niece bought some cookies a week prior and sent a check for over the due amount. You guessed it, two dollars even.

I covered for my friend and God covered for me. There's no greater love than this.

Lemon Sandwich Cookies

1. **1 cup refined organic coconut oil, melted***
2. **½ cup organic sugar (Wholesome Sweeteners)**
3. **½ cup organic sucanat (Wholesome Sweeteners)**
4. **2 tablespoons flaxseeds (Bob's Red Mill)**
5. **⅓ cup rice milk**
6. **2 teaspoons lemon peel**
7. **2 tablespoons freshly squeezed lemon juice**
8. **2 teaspoons lemon oil (Simply Organic)**
9. **1 cup amaranth flour (Bob's Red Mill)**
10. **1 tablespoon arrowroot starch (Bob's Red Mill)**
11. **½ teaspoon sea salt (Real Salt)**
12. **½ teaspoon baking soda**
13. **3½ cups gluten-free oats (Bob's Red Mill), finely ground****

$\mathcal{T}$urn mixer on and slowly combine ingredients 1 through 5 in order, then mix for 1 minute on medium high speed (mixture will have "glazed" appearance). Add ingredients 6 through 8, and mix on medium high for 1 minute. Gradually add amaranth flour and mix well, scraping sides when needed. Add ingredients 10 through 12, and mix well. Gradually add oat flour on medium high for 1 to 2 minutes. You cannot over-mix this mixture.

*Melt coconut oil in saucepan on low heat, then add to mixer.

**Making oat flour: Grind 3½ cups oats in food processor or flour mill. This will yield approximately 2½ cups oat flour.

Place soft dough in plastic sealed container and refrigerate for 2 to 3 hours until dough is solid.

Preheat oven to 375°F. Roll dough ½-inch thick on floured surface. To prevent dough from sticking to rolling pin, spray canola oil spray on rolling pin. Cut with 2½-inch round cookie cutter. Place cookies on parchment paper on cookie sheet about 2 inches apart.

Bake for 10 to 12 minutes. Baking time depends on thickness and size of cookie. (Bottom of cookie will be slightly browned.)

Cool cookies for 1 hour. Spread lemon icing on cookie and assemble another cookie on top. To add extra decoration, dip them in powdered sugar. See page 82 for icing recipe.

Refrigerate to ensure freshness. Store these cookies in a tightly sealed container lined with parchment paper. These cookies freeze well, too.

Makes 32 large cookies using a 2½-inch cookie cutter.

Note: We utilize organic ingredients when available.

*V*ariation: Try this variation with Lemon, Chocolate or Vanilla Icing.

Vanilla Chocolate Sandwich Cookies

1. **1 cup refined organic coconut oil, melted**
2. ½ cup organic sugar (Wholesome Sweeteners)
3. ½ cup organic sucanat (Wholesome Sweeteners)
4. **2 tablespoons flaxseeds** (Bob's Red Mill)
5. ½ cup rice milk
6. **1 tablespoon vanilla extract** (Simply Organic)
7. **1 cup amaranth flour** (Bob's Red Mill)
8. **2 tablespoons arrowroot**
9. ½ teaspoon salt (Real Salt)
10. ½ teaspoon baking soda
11. **3½ cups gluten-free oats, finely ground***

$\mathcal{T}$urn on mixer and gradually add ingredients 1 through 6 in order, then mix for 2 minutes on medium high (mixture will have a "glazed" appearance). Add ingredients 7 through 10 on medium high for 1 minute, scraping bowl occasionally. Gradually add oats and mix on medium high for 1 to 2 minutes. You cannot over-mix this mixture.

Place soft dough in plastic sealed container and refrigerate for 2 to 3 hours until dough is solid.

To prevent dough from sticking to a rolling pin, spray canola oil on rolling pin.

Preheat oven to 375°F. Roll dough ½-inch thick on floured surface. Cut with 2½ inch-round cookie cutter. Place cookies on parchment paper about 2 inches apart.

Bake for 10 to 12 minutes. Baking time depends on thickness and size of cookie. Bottom of cookie will be slightly browned.

Cool cookies for 1 hour. Spread chocolate icing on cookie and assemble a vanilla cookie on top. To add extra decoration, dip them in powdered sugar. See page 82 for icing recipe.

Refrigerate to ensure freshness. Store these cookies with lined parchment paper in a tightly sealed container. They freeze very well, too.

Note: We utilize organic ingredients when available.

"A gift opens the way for the giver and ushers him into the presence of the great."
Proverbs 18:6 (NJV)

Gifts from the Kitchen, Gifts from the Heart

*I*magine my disappointment when my brother Dan and sister Mellody called to tell me about our parents' 50th anniversary party. Given our dire financial situation, I knew airplane tickets for three people to Dallas, Texas were out of the question. I wanted God to miraculously provide the travel money necessary to witness mom and dad's marriage milestone, but He didn't. Instead, my role in the affair was to bake from home.

Making healthy desserts for the 60 guests would be our contribution to help make the event memorable. I knew my parents would appreciate the gift, having enjoyed my baked goods in the past. My other brother Joe called to place an order for his favorite desserts, carob and chocolate brownies. I spent hours baking those brownies and an assortment of other treats, individually wrapping each one and packaging them in a beautiful display to showcase our love.

After the party, we received an outpouring of thanks. The desserts helped make the celebration special and were an engaging conversation piece. Most people had never used the words "healthy" and "delicious" in the same sentence when talking about chocolate brownies.

To most of the partygoers, my presence was felt through the work of my hands. But the ultimate compliment came from my mom. As only a mom can do, she acknowledged the desserts weren't just treats from my kitchen, but gifts from my heart.

Chocolate Cake Brownies

1. ¾ cup canola oil
2. ¾ cup honey
3. 1¼ cups rice milk
4. ¼ cup flaxseed meal (Bob's Red Mill)
5. 2 teaspoons vanilla extract (Simply Organic)
6. 1½ cups brown rice flour (Bob's Red Mill)
7. ½ cup organic amaranth flour (Bob's Red Mill)
8. 1 cup organic cocoa powder (Now® Foods)
9. 1 teaspoon baking soda
10. ¾ teaspoon sea salt (Real Salt)
11. 2 teaspoons baking powder
12. 1 cup organic walnuts, minced
13. ½ cup semi-sweet chocolate baking chips (Enjoy Life)
    Canola cooking spray

Preheat oven to 350°F. Spray 9 x 13-inch pan with canola oil. Combine ingredients 1 through 5 (add in order), and mix for 2 minutes on medium high speed. Gradually blend in ingredients 6 through 8 (add in order), and mix on medium speed, scraping bowl occasionally. Add ingredients 9 through 11 (in order), and mix on medium high speed for 1 minute. Add walnuts and chocolate chips, and mix on medium high speed for 1 minute.

Pour into pan. Bake for 18 to 20 minutes. Cool for 1 hour.

Family Tip: To ensure a smooth cut, spray canola oil on knife before cutting brownies.

Topping suggestions: Fresh strawberries, our Homemade Chocolate Syrup (see recipe below), a scoop of vanilla non-dairy ice cream or all of the above for a deluxe brownie delight!

Our Family's Homemade Chocolate Syrup:
¾ cup semi-sweet chocolate baking chips (Enjoy Life)
¼ cup rice milk

Place baking chips in double boiler. When chips are melted, turn off stove top and add ¼ cup rice milk. Drizzle on brownie!

Note: We utilize organic ingredients when available.

"I will never leave you nor forsake you."
Joshua 1:5 (NIV)

Life Lesson
from Happy Joe

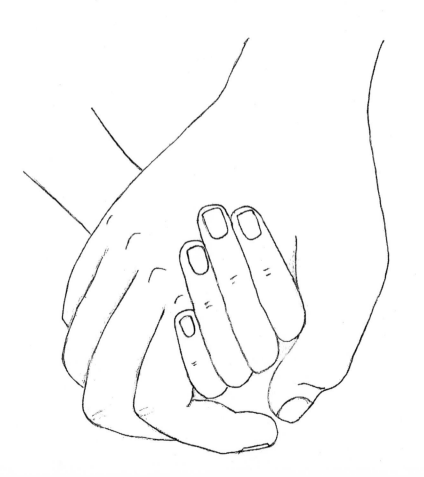

Aptly known to Alexander as "Happy Joe" because of his eternal smile, my mentally challenged brother underwent surgery several years ago to remove a 28-year-old brain tumor. Joe's doctors were amazed he had done so well through the years.

Before the surgery, I called to offer him an incentive to fight hard and not give up. Ron and I wanted him to visit us in Georgia after he had recovered. He was thrilled to have the opportunity to travel from Texas to Georgia: "I'll be coming to visit you. You can count on it."

Thankfully, the surgery to remove the benign mass was a success. A couple of weeks later, Joe called to make good on our offer. I made special arrangements with the airline for his care because of his mental challenges and medical condition. At my request, an airline representative was to wait with Joe at the gate until Alexander and I arrived. Somehow in the confusion of multiple gate changes, he was released into the massive landscape of the world's busiest airport, Hartsfield-Jackson Atlanta International Airport.

I called my sister and friends and asked them to pray we would find Joe. With airport security on our "search and rescue" team, we frantically combed the airport. We explored the terrain searching for Joe on terminal trains, moving sidewalks, elevators, and escalators.

For security reasons, Alexander, who was only three years old at the time, needed to be carried. I was physically exhausted toting a toddler on our quest.

After a three-hour search, a security officer approached me with the words I longed to hear. "We found Joe!" With Alexander in my arms, I ran through the terminal toward the security office where Joe calmly waited. He looked up at us with his "Happy Joe" smile. Breathlessly I said, "We've looked everywhere for you! We were so worried about you!" No explanations or excuses were made. All he said in return was, "I knew you would never leave me Sharon. That don't make sense."

Although the search to find Joe ended, the lesson it taught me remains today. God used my brother to remind me of God's promise to "never leave or forsake us" no matter what we do or how far we roam. That's how deeply He loves. It wouldn't make sense otherwise. I, too, was lost, but now I'm found. Thank God His word is true.

My brother loves carob and brownies, so these are for you, "Happy Joe!"

Carob Sunflower Brownies

1. ¾ cup organic canola oil
2. ¾ cup honey
3. ¾ cup rice milk
4. ¼ cup flaxseed meal (Bob's Red Mill)
5. 2 teaspoons vanilla (Simply Organic)
6. 1½ cups brown rice flour
   (Bob's Red Mill)
7. 1 teaspoon baking soda
8. ¾ teaspoon sea salt (Real Salt)
9. ¾ cup sunflower butter
10. 1 cup unsweetened carob powder
11. ½ cup raw sunflower seeds
12. ½ cup carob baking chips
    Canola cooking spray

𝒫reheat oven to 350°F. Spray 9 x 13-inch pan with canola oil. Combine ingredients 1 through 5 (add in order), and mix for 1 minute on medium high speed. Gradually blend in ingredients 6 through 8 (add in order), and mix on medium speed, scraping bowl occasionally. Add ingredients 9 and 10 (in order), and mix on medium high speed for 1 minute until well blended. Add sunflower seeds on medium speed.

Spread batter evenly into pan (batter will be thick). Swirl carob baking chips on top of batter.

Bake for 18 to 20 minutes.

Cool for 1 hour. Cut brownies and refrigerate.

Note: We utilize organic ingredients when available.

"A man of many companions may come to ruin, but there is a friend who sticks closer than a brother." Proverbs 18:24 (NJV)

Comfort Food
Made with Love

$\mathcal{W}$hen I see friends going through a tough time, I do what comes naturally to me. I bake. My love, support and concern are intangible ingredients in each "friendship batch" I share. From my experience, I've come to learn acts of love are more appreciated and useful than words easily padded with platitudes. During overwhelming life decisions and situations, saying "everything will be OK" to the cross bearer may not sound like empathetic words of love.

A faraway friend was in the middle of such a life crisis. Our distance limited the amount of emotional support I could provide, so in lieu of my shoulder to cry on, I sent her some Petite Chocolate Cakes. Perhaps she could find a little comfort in some comfort food.

She called to say the cakes, accompanied by her tea and Bible, helped nourish her spirit as she sat down to ponder her major life decision. She felt comfort knowing her friend had poured so much love into making such decadent, yet healthy cakes. Later, she sent me an enthusiastic endorsement:

> "How many times have we sunk our teeth into a luscious slice of chocolate cake with a tinge of guilt? Well, kiss your guilt goodbye! Introducing the absolutely guilt-free chocolate cake. This cake is so nourishing you can eat it for breakfast, lunch and dinner. It's that good for you. Can you believe it? Finally, a chocolate cake that nourishes your body. Lose the guilt and gain your favorite new luscious chocolate extravagance!"

I chuckled thinking how these cakes inspired her beyond their intended purpose to provide comfort and love from one friend to another. Acts of love create unbreakable bonds.

Petite Chocolate Cakes or Cupcakes

1. ¾ cup canola oil
2. ¾ cup honey
3. 1 cup rice milk
4. ¼ cup flaxseed meal (Bob's Red Mill)
5. ¾ teaspoon sea salt (Real Salt)
6. 2 teaspoons vanilla extract (Simply Organic)
7. 1½ cups brown rice flour (Bob's Red Mill)
8. ½ cup organic amaranth flour (Bob's Red Mill)
9. 1 cup organic unsweetened cocoa powder (Now® Foods)
10. 1 teaspoon baking soda
11. 2 teaspoons baking powder
12. ½ cup semi-sweet chocolate chips (Enjoy Life)

Preheat oven to 350°F. Line petite loaf pans with petite baking cups. Mix ingredients 1 through 5 (add in order) for 1 minute on medium high speed. Gradually blend in ingredients 6 through 8 (add in order), and mix on medium speed for 1 minute, scraping bowl occasionally. Add ingredients 9 through 11 (in order), and mix on medium high speed for 1 to 2 minutes, scraping bowl occasionally. Add baking chips and mix into batter.

Pour into petite bread pans. (You can buy petite bread mold pans and petite baking liners at Hobby Lobby. Wilton brand pans hold 9 petite bread molds.) An ice cream scoop works well to put batter in pans.

Bake for 13 to 15 minutes. Cool for 1 hour. Decorate when cakes are cooled. See page 82 for vanilla or chocolate icing recipe.

Makes approximately 18 petite cakes. These make lovely gifts!

For cupcake variation:
Fill each about ¾ full. Bake cupcakes for 15 to 18 minutes, until wooden pick or cake tester inserted in cupcakes comes out clean.

Note: We utilize organic ingredients when available.

"Let the wise listen and add to their learning."
Proverbs 1:5 (NJV)

The Layers of Life

$\mathcal{A}$lexander turned three years old before he got to blow out candles on his third birthday cake. It was far from traditional cake with all the substitutions needed to make it safe for my little boy, but it was a cake nonetheless and just as tasty.

When I asked Alexander what kind of cake he wanted, he blurted, "A big chocolate cake!" I realized then it was time to get to work creating the recipe for this non-existent "big chocolate cake." After many experiments with the special ingredients, the cake evolved into an exceptional treat.

$\mathcal{T}rust$...

As I decorated the Three-Layer Chocolate Cake, I reflected on life lessons we had learned with Alexander over the past three years of his life. The first layer of the cake was a metaphor for learning to trust. It was hard to understand, much less accept, why our little boy had to endure so much pain as a result of severe food allergies and skin afflictions. When would he be healed? Would he? God said, "Trust me and I will make a path for his healing." Trying to maintain control over our circumstances wasn't an option. It was an exhausting and futile waste of time. We learned to trust through surrender.

Listen...

I stacked the next layer on the cake and thought about learning to listen.
We prayed for guidance during Alexander's early struggles when he couldn't
eat anything without causing a breakout. The encouraging words in
Proverbs 1:4 gave us hope: "Let the wise listen and add to their learning."
God taught us to listen for direction. We precariously followed His path
for Alexander's healing.

Believe...

The third and final layer represented what results from learning to trust
and listen. You learn to believe. Belief chokes doubt out of seemingly insur-
mountable situations. Jesus said "If you have faith as small as a mustard
seed, you can say to this mountain, 'Move' and it will move. Nothing will be
impossible for you." (Matthew 17:20) I stood back and looked at these layers
with deep gratitude for all the experiences, good and bad, that had led us to
unabashedly follow God.

Now, more than four years after blowing out the candles on that cake,
I see more clearly what happens when you trust, listen and believe.
Mountains move!

Three-Layer Chocolate Cake

*M*any hours have been lovingly devoted to experimenting with this recipe to perfect its taste. This chocolate cake has been enjoyed by many family members, friends and customers. Try this recipe for your next celebration!

1. 1½ cups canola oil
2. 1½ cups honey
3. 2¼ cups rice milk
4. ½ cup flaxseed meal (Bob's Red Mill)
5. 2 teaspoons vanilla extract (Simply Organic)
6. 3 cups brown rice flour (Bob's Red Mill)
7. 2 teaspoons baking soda
8. 1½ teaspoons sea salt (Real Salt)
9. 1 tablespoon plus 1 teaspoon baking powder
10. 1 cup amaranth flour (Bob's Red Mill)
11. 2 cups organic cocoa powder (Now® Foods)

Optional:
12. 2 cups organic walnuts, minced
13. 1 cup semi-sweet chocolate baking chips (Enjoy Life)
    Canola cooking spray

*P*reheat oven to 350°F. Prepare baking pans (3 pans measuring 9 inches in diameter by 1½ inches deep) by cutting out parchment paper to fit bottoms of pans. Spray parchment-lined pans lightly with canola oil. Mix ingredients 1 through 5 (add in order) for 1 minute on medium high speed. Gradually blend in ingredients 6 through 9 (add in order), and mix on medium speed, scraping bowl occasionally. Add ingredients 10 and 11 (in order), and mix on medium high speed for 1 minute. Add walnuts and mix on medium low. Add baking chips and mix on low speed.

Pour batter evenly into the 3 pans.

Bake for 18 to 20 minutes, until wooden pick or cake tester is inserted in middle of cake and comes out fairly clean. To ensure moistness, do not overbake. Set pans on cooling rack for 1 hour. Please note: The cake will not have a traditional "fluffy" look. When the 3 layers are stacked and iced it will look like a traditional chocolate cake.

Icing the Three-Layer Cake (see page 82 for icing recipe):

Cool cake completely before removing from pans.

Family Tip: Place a glass of warm water with a knife next to icing. Insert knife in water for the icing to spread easier.

Place first layer upside down on decorating plate or cake pedestal. Place this layer in freezer for about 30 minutes (this will prevent crumbs.) Take first layer out of freezer and spread room temperature icing on side and top of cake. This will help seal crumbs. Add second layer and spread room temperature icing on side and top of cake. Place third layer on top without icing and place in freezer for about 1 hour. Remove and finish icing cake.

Natural decorating ideas: 1) Sprinkle ground walnuts on top; 2) Cover cake with dehydrated coconut slices and place strawberries on top in the center.

Note: We utilize organic ingredients when available.

Sharon's Icing Recipes

Family Tip: The butter in these recipes contains soy. For those who need to avoid soy, try using goat butter or palm oil for substitutes.

Vanilla Icing

- ¾ cup non-dairy butter (Earth Balance®, "buttery sticks")
- 7 cups sifted powdered sugar (Wholesome Sweeteners)
- ½ cup rice milk
- 1½ teaspoon vanilla extract (Simply Organic)

Mix butter on medium high speed until creamy. Gradually add sifted powdered sugar, rice milk and vanilla, occasionally scraping bowl. Mix ingredients on high speed until creamy.

Chocolate Icing

- ¾ cup non-dairy butter (Earth Balance®, "buttery sticks")
- 7 cups sifted powdered sugar (Wholesome Sweeteners)
- ½ cup sifted unsweetened cocoa powder (Now® Foods)
- ½ cup rice milk
- 2 teaspoons vanilla extract (Simply Organic)

Mix butter on medium high speed until creamy. Gradually add sifted powdered sugar and rice milk on medium high speed. Gradually add cocoa and vanilla. Mix ingredients on high speed until creamy.

Lemon Icing
- ½ cup non-dairy butter (Earth Balance®)
- 4½ cups sifted powdered sugar (Wholesome Sweeteners)
- 1 tablespoon lemon juice (1 lemon, squeezed)
- ¼ cup rice milk
- 2 teaspoons lemon oil (Simply Organic)
- 1 teaspoon lemon zest (grate outside of lemon)

Mix butter on medium high speed until creamy. Gradually add sifted powdered sugar, rice milk, lemon juice, lemon oil and lemon zest. Mix ingredients on high speed until creamy.

No-Powdered-Sugar Icing
Chocolate Coconut Icing
- ½ cup raw honey
- ¼ cup non-dairy butter (Earth Balance®,"buttery sticks")
- 1 cup sifted unsweetened cocoa powder (Now® Foods)
- 2 tablespoons rice milk
- 1 teaspoon vanilla extract (Simply Organic)
- 2 tablespoons coconut flour (Bob's Red Mill)

Mix butter on medium high speed until creamy. Gradually add honey and cocoa, occasionally scraping the bowl. Add rice milk, vanilla and coconut flour.

Health Benefits from Our Recipes

$\mathcal{T}$he recipes in this cookbook are gluten-free, egg-free and dairy-free. However, there are some people with celiac disease, allergies or compromised immune systems, who are unable to tolerate gluten-free oats. Please consult your health care physician with questions or concerns regarding ingredients of which you are unsure.

The recipes were created for Alexander, family, friends and customers who focused on healthy eating or needed special dietary care. A key "ingredient" was to add as many "healthy benefits" to each recipe. We hope that you are excited to know that with every bite of every item you bake, it is bursting with nutrition!

FLOURS

Amaranth Flour Of all grains, amaranth has the highest protein content, and is a good source of calcium, fiber and iron.

Brown Rice Flour Brown rice is high in fiber and provides vitamins and minerals such as potassium, thiamin, niacin and iron.

Coconut Flour Very high in fiber, low in digestible carbohydrates, a good source of protein.

Oats/Oat Flour Full of protein, thiamine, riboflavin, niacin, iron, calcium, phosphorus, sodium and potassium.

Tapioca Flour Tapioca comes from the Cassava plant. The Cassava is comparable to potatoes, except that it has twice the fiber content and a higher level of potassium.

FRUIT

Apricots Contain magnesium, iron, beta-carotene, potassium and calcium.

Bananas Contain Vitamin C, potassium, fiber and Vitamin B6.

Raspberries An excellent source of Vitamin C.

OILS

Canola Oil A monounsaturated fat oil obtained from the seed of a plant related to mustard. Contains Omega-3 fatty acids.

Coconut Oil Sources of essential fatty acids. These oils typically contain the following beneficial fatty acids: lauric acid, myristic acid, caprylic acid, capric acid, oleic acid and linoleic acid.

Olive Oil Contain polyunsaturated fat, monounsaturated fat, Omega-3 fatty acids, Omega-6, Vitamin E and Vitamin K.

SEEDS AND NUTS

Flaxseed/Flaxseed meal
Flax oil derived from flax seeds is one of the highest known sources of soluble fiber, magnesium, zinc and linolenic acid (an Omega-3 fatty acid). The Omega-3 content of the oil is typically 52%. Flax seeds also provide protein, mucilage, phytosterol and plant lignans.

Pecans A good source for a number of nutrients, including zinc and magnesium. They are also a good source of fiber.

Sunflower Seeds Raw sunflower seeds provide a wealth of important nutrients. They are an excellent source of Vitamin E, magnesium, and copper. They also provide iron, zinc, and some calcium. They are low in saturated fat and are a good source of dietary fiber.

Walnuts Versatile treat and a good source of magnesium, fiber and protein. They are also low in saturated fat but high in Omega-3 fats.

NATURAL SWEETENERS

Agave Organic blue agave is a natural sweetener extracted from the core of the blue agave plant. With a glycemic index of 39 or less, it provides natural sweetness without the blood sugar spike.

Carob A legume that comes from the dried pods of the carob tree, which is a healthy substitute for chocolate. It provides protein and B vitamins.

Cocoa Here are some facts about Now® Foods Cocoa Powder: Each 55 calorie serving (1/4 cup) contains 2.25 grams of fat, just over 11 grams of carbohydrates, 6.5 grams of dietary fiber, 325 mg of potassium and

5 grams of protein. Each serving of NOW® non-alkalinized Organic Cocoa Powder contains 21.5 - 107.5 mg of cocoa flavanols (polyphenols).

Honey Vitamins and minerals including traces of riboflavin (B12), niacin (B3), pantothenic acid (B5), Vitamin B6, Folate (B9), Vitamin C, calcium, iron, magnesium, phosphorus, potassium, zinc.

Organic Sugar Evaporated cane juice.

Sucanat Dehydrated cane juice.

Nutritional Resources:
Bob's Red Mill, Wholesome Sweeteners and Now® Foods
These nutritional facts are provided for educational purposes only, and not to treat, diagnosis, or cure any disease.

Our Family's Favorite Brands

The recipes created in this book have been made utilizing these brands. We love these companies and we are offering these options to assist you in finding the proper ingredients.

These companies have not paid us to endorse them. We promote them knowing they make quality products that you can trust.

Bob's Red Mill
13521 SE Pheasant Court
Milwaukie, OR 97222
1.800.349.2173
www.bobsredmill.com

Cascadian Farm
Small Planet Foods
P.O. Box 9452
Minneapolis, MN 55440
1.800.624.4123
www.cascadianfarm.com

Earth Balance®
Owned & Disturbed by:
GFA Brands Inc.
Paramus, NJ 07652-1432
201.568.9300
www.earthbalancenatural.com

Enjoy Life
3810 River Rd.
Schiller Park, IL 60176
1.888.50.ENJOY
www.enjoylifefoods.com

Frontier Natural Products
Co-op/Simply Organic
PO Box 299
3021 78th St.
Norway, IA 52318
1.800.669.3275
www.frontiercoop.com

Garden of Life
770 Northpoint Parkway, Suite 100
West Palm Beach, FL 33407
866.465.0051
www.gardenoflife.com

Now® Foods
395 S. Glen Ellyn Rd.
Bloomingdale, IL 60108
1.888.669.3663
www.nowfoods.com

Real Salt
Redmond Trading Company, L.C.
475 West 910 South
Heber City, UT 84032
1.800.367.7258
www.realsalt.com

Redwood Hill Farm & Creamery
2064 Highway 116 North
Building 1, Suite 130
Sebastopol, CA 95472
707.823.8250
www.redwoodshill.com

Whole Foods Market, Inc.
550 Bowie Street
Austin, TX 78703
512.477.4455
www.wholefoodsmarket.com

Wholesome Sweeteners
8016 Highway 90-A
Sugarland, TX 77478
1.800.680.1896
www.organicsugrs.biz

Note: Whole Foods Market
merchandises all the brands
listed here. To find a location
near you, please see their website.

Final Thoughts

from Sharon

Our mission is to help people live a joyful life "healthy from the inside out™." "Examine me, God...Make sure I'm fit inside and out so I never lose sight of your love, but keep in step with you, never missing a beat." Psalm 26: 2-3 (The Message™). I hope that the stories in this book have inspired and encouraged you. I pray you will experience all the blessings and miracles that come from a magnificent God when you "Trust, Listen and Believe!"

Great blessings to you!

from Alexander

Thank you for buying our book. Hope you liked the stories and recipes. Eat more cookies!

We would love to hear your encouraging stories.
Please feel free to write us:

Ron, Sharon and Alexander Feskanin
P.O. Box 544
Alpharetta, GA 30009-0544

Also, please check out our website, www.zandershealthybakery.com